TRENDING

HOW and WHY STUFF GETS POPULAR

By Kira Vermond

Illustrated by Clayton Hanmer

Owlkids Books

For Katie and her bell-bottomed jeans, sporting a butterfly patch. (Tag. You're it.) — K.V.

To my beautiful wife and daughter, jogging pants and flower dresses will always be in style in my heart! — CTON

Owlkids Books acknowledges the financial support of the Canada Council for the Arts, the Ontario Arts Council, the Government of Canada through the Canada Book Fund (CBF) and the Government of Ontario through the Ontario Creates Book Initiative for our publishing activities.

Published in Canada by
Owlkids Books Inc.
1 Eglinton Avenue East
Toronto, ON M4P 3A1

Published in the United States by
Owlkids Books Inc.
1700 Fourth Street
Berkeley, CA 94710

Library and Archives Canada Cataloguing in Publication

Title: Trending : how and why stuff gets popular / by Kira Vermond ; illustrated by Clayton Hanmer.
Names: Vermond, Kira, author. | Hanmer, Clayton, 1978- illustrator.
Description: Includes bibliographical references and index.
Identifiers: Canadiana 20190127074 | ISBN 9781771473255 (hardcover)
Subjects: LCSH: Fads—Juvenile literature. | LCSH: Popular culture—Juvenile literature.
Classification: LCC HM621 .V47 2020 | DDC j306—dc23

Library of Congress Control Number: 2019947225

Edited by Karen Li and Katherine Dearlove
Designed by Barb Kelly

Thank You Kindly

Being a writer is one of the best jobs in the world, but books are a lot of (fun) work! The reason *Trending* exists at all is because so many people worked together to make it happen. Thank you, Karen Li and Katherine Dearlove, for your thoughtful edits and patience! Clayton Hanmer, you're a (humble) genius, dude. Barb Kelly for the spiffy design work. Nicole, Andy, and The Bookshelf, thanks for the quiet workspace. Jean Mills and Lisa Dalrymple, you're the best book idea listeners ever. But most of all, I'm so thankful for the input of my amazing kid writers: Annika, Asha, Beatrice, Daniel, Francesca, Jaya, Katie, Kiran, Leo, Leopold, Nola, Nadia, Sierra, Stella, and Zola. And Dave, Nathan, and Nadia? You're the opposite of a fad. True classics. I'll love you forever.

Manufactured in Guangzhou, Dongguan, China, in October 2019, by Toppan Leefung Packaging & Printing (Dongguan) Co., Ltd. Job #BAYDC66

A   B   C   D   E   F

 Publisher of Chirp, Chickadee and OWL
www.owlkidsbooks.com | Owlkids Books is a division of bayard canada

CONTENTS

What fad are you into right now?

Counting jelly beans? Wearing your socks inside out? Collecting dryer lint? (Jean lint is worth way more than white underwear lint. Everybody knows that.) Some bizarre fads rise and fall so quickly, they might be over by the time you've finished reading this book!

INTRODUCTION

Would you ever...

Swallow a live goldfish?

Spend a whopping $10,000 on a stuffed animal?

Dance for nine hundred hours straight?

Pour a bucketful of ice water over your head?

Eat nothing but cabbage soup for weeks?

Run naked through a crowd of complete strangers?

You're probably shaking your head. There's no way you'd ever do any of those things. Who the heck would?

Yet, for centuries, regular people just like you have made some pretty irregular decisions in order to follow the latest craze or fad. (All of these ones really did happen, by the way. Even the one involving the ill-fated goldfish. Gulp.)

But here's the thing. While most fads might seem just silly or trivial on the surface, dig a little deeper and you'll see they **can have major, far-reaching, and long-term impacts on our lives**—and even on those who live far away.

Here's a classic example ripped straight from the history books: **beaver felt hats**.

Leave It to Beavers

Hats crafted from felted beaver pelts (skins) once swept across Europe as the latest fashion craze. By the 17th century, everybody had to have them!

Only one problem. Nearly all the beavers in Europe had already been hunted to extinction. In order to keep up with growing demand, trappers set off for North America.

Things just got worse for beavers. So many were killed in North America—ten to fifteen *million* in the 1700s alone—that they were nearly wiped out!

Without beavers to dam waterways, many ponds and marshes dried up. Ducks flew away. Muskrat and otter homes froze or flooded. Marshes became meadows, and minks and raccoons no longer had tasty water-loving frogs and snakes to eat. Ecosystems went belly-up.

When the traders ran low on their furry supply, they pushed farther and farther into the territories of North America's Indigenous people. Traders from France and Great Britain allied themselves at various times with the Wendat, the Algonquian, and the Haudenosaunee, among other groups. Fighting broke out in the 17th century over the best beaver-filled lands—what's now known as the Beaver Wars. It became one of the bloodiest conflicts in North American history. Between war and diseases introduced by the settlers, entire Indigenous communities were wiped out.

See? One fashion fad in faraway Europe

• changed ecosystems;

• shaped the creation of new countries;

• started wars;

• and disrupted, even destroyed, communities and traditional ways of life.

Fads, trends, and crazes have existed throughout our history…well up until today. But how exactly do they spread from person to person, town to town, and even country to country—and why do we follow the herd in the first place?

WHAT MAKES A FAD A FAD?

You probably know one when you see one: a seemingly random toy, game, fashion, or song that suddenly becomes the NEXT BIG THING! But what exactly makes it a fad and not something else? What characteristics do fads have? This chapter gives the lowdown on their defining features so you'll be able to spot them a mile away.

BUT FIRST...

Featuring: The Thing You've Always Wanted (Since Last Week)

Raj has one. So does Ava. You want one, too! Only one teensy-weensy problem...

Some say kids in Japan were doing it first, but others are sure they saw it pop up in Sweden ages ago...

Wherever it came from, it's taking your country by storm. Some people are fighting over it!

Even your grandma wants to give it a whirl!

This thing is sooo great!

Now a brand-new industry is cashing in on the craze.

!?!

But some experts are skeptical it's here to stay.

It serves no purpose. It even tastes bad! I give it another couple of months...until the next hot thing comes along.

Q: Can you guess which fad this is?

A: Does it matter? Nearly every craze, fad, rage, or obsession follows a similar pattern that lifts it from obscurity and slingshots it to stardom.

So what exactly does a fad's life cycle look like?

Turn the page to find out...

7

DIFFERENT FADS, SAME PATTERN

Here's the Story:

CROCS

They're springy, comfortable, and marshmallow-light, but yowzers, are they ugly!

Enter Crocs, the footwear fashion faux pas that put a spring in the step of millions of kids and adults around the world. Maybe you have an old pair stuffed in the back of your closet. (Or even worse, your *mom* does.)

What started as a light and waterproof boating shoe surged to popularity after an American company invented a funny name (from the side, the shoes look like smiling crocodiles) and started selling the colorful foam clogs. In 2002, Crocs earned only $1,000 in profit.

Then, BOOM!

By 2007, the Crocs company was selling an astounding $847 million worth of shoes a year, covering more than forty countries. Celebrities were spotted wearing them, little kids adorned them with plastic charms —and eventually copycat businesses started selling knockoffs, too.

Sure, Crocs are comfortable— just don't look down

But in 2008, the other shoe dropped. It was as though everyone suddenly woke up, looked down at their feet, and screamed!

Enter...the backlash.

"They've spread like an infection to the farthest reaches of the globe," read one shoe-bashing website, ihatecrocs.com. "Consumers worldwide are abandoning their dignity…"

8

Soon newspaper stories were running critical headlines, such as "Croc Horror!" and "Crocs Can Kill!" A few wearers—mostly little kids—were seriously injured when their Crocs got trapped at the end of escalators. Some hospitals banned them, citing worries that the hole-covered clogs wouldn't protect their medical staff from sharp objects and spills.

The company soon lost millions of dollars and laid off about two thousand workers. The fad was over. But a comeback is always possible.

WHAT DOES IT ALL MEAN?

True fads have a beginning, a middle, and a definite end. They seem to come out of nowhere. And here's something else all fads have in common: they generate a lot of energy and enthusiasm in a very short period of time. This life cycle doesn't last long either. Think weeks or months, not years or decades.

If we were to graph the life span of a fad, it would look like this:

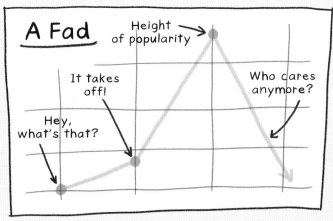

Now take a look at how much the Crocs company was worth over the course of the fad.

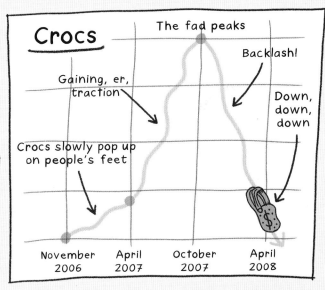

See? Always the same pattern. If you know what to look out for, you'll find that fads are incredibly predictable!

THE FASTER THEY RISE, THE HARDER THEY FALL

Here's the Story: POKÉMON GO

It was 2016—what some people called "the summer of *Pokémon Go*."

In early July, *millions* of people downloaded an app, a game based on popular Japanese trading cards from the '90s. Soon players were wandering around neighborhoods looking for ways to catch virtual monsters with their phones.

The game was so hot it spread around the world in a matter of days.

Pokémon pandemonium!

Although the game was tons of fun—and sent kids and adults outside for plenty of sunshine and exercise—there were side effects. For instance, hundreds of people would suddenly show up at a single location to capture Squirtles and Charizards.

This was a real problem at already-busy locations. Gamers were trampling park flower beds, littering, and causing confusion. Officials worried about safety. Some players tried to capture digital monsters while driving, running into traffic, or—eek!—during funerals at cemeteries.

HONK!

PRIVATE

DO NOT ENTER!

Eventually, city governments decided they had to step in. Toronto asked the game developer to move digital Pokéstops away from its busy downtown ferry terminal. The state of Illinois had a similar problem when heavy foot traffic destroyed rare plant life in a Chicago conservation area.

KEEP OUT!

Then, nearly as quickly as the fad started, *Pokémon Go*'s popularity dropped. By the end of August (when many kids headed back to school), the red-hot game flamed out.

WHAT DOES IT ALL MEAN?

The *Pokémon Go* fad is a perfect example of what happens when something takes off at lightning speed. In fact, just days after its launch, news headlines predicted "*Pokémon Go* Fad Will Be Gone by Christmas." They were right. At its peak, there were 28.5 million users in the United States alone. By the end of 2016, only five million players were still trying to "catch 'em all."

A flash-in-the-pan craze can actually become too popular for its own good. That's what some U.S. and Spanish researchers discovered in 2009, when they looked at how fads work: The rise and fall of a fad actually mirror each other. If something takes off like a shot—which happens more often in the Internet age, by the way—it's more likely to crash and burn quickly, too. The flip side is true as well. Something that takes a while to become popular is likely to remain popular longer.

So, sure, you might dream that a game you invent becomes an overnight sensation, but hold your horses! If you want it to last, just hope it doesn't become too popular *too* quickly! Slow and steady is the key to long-lasting success.

I WANT IT BECAUSE I CAN'T HAVE IT!

Here's the Story:
HULA-HOOPS

There was the Spin-a-Hoop, Hoop Zing, and Hooper Dooper. But you probably know these lightweight plastic rings by another name: Hula-Hoop.

Back in 1958, a plastic hoop fad hit North America, and it's still considered one of the biggest, wildest, and most intense fads ever. Selling for $1.98, Hula-Hoops, created by Wham-O Inc., were cheap, colorful, and easy to master in five minutes flat.

But there was a problem: The hoops were nothing special to look at. Could kids be convinced to try them? The company sent employees to California playgrounds to give demonstrations. Hula-Hoops also appeared on TV.

Success! Everyone had to have a hoop. Moms, dads, kids, and grandparents were taking them for a spin. There were timed contests. "The Hula-Hoop Song" became a Top 40 hit. Other toy companies even jumped in, helping launch a whole new lightweight-plastics industry.

WHAT DOES IT ALL MEAN?

Sure, swinging a ring around your torso for ten minutes is *kind* of fun, but so is stargazing, going on scavenger hunts, and drawing unflattering pictures of your teacher. So why exactly did the Hula-Hoop become so popular so quickly?

One main reason: **supply** and **demand**.

What's that?

Supply: How much of something is available.

Demand: How much of something people want.

When supply and demand are the same—there are enough Hula-Hoops to go around but not too many—we call that **equilibrium**.

Wham-O Inc. had brilliant marketing people who knew how to manipulate supply and demand. Not only were they good at advertising their hoops, they were also really good at figuring out what people would pay for a hoop to create that equilibrium. At $1.98, the Hula-Hoop was the perfect price.

Twenty-five million Wham-O hoops were sold in only a few months at the height of the craze, and the company made $45 million in profit. Wham-O Inc. had dozens of factories running at full tilt, churning out thousands of plastic hoops each day.

Sometimes, though, they sold out and demand went through the roof!

All sold out

When demand is greater than supply, equilibrium goes bust! Stores have too many buyers and not enough hoops to sell. The toys suddenly seem more valuable.

It's a flood!

Too much demand encourages copycat companies who also want to cash in. And when thousands of copycat hoops turned up in stores, there was too much supply, and hoops no longer seemed as special.

By November 1958, the hoop fad faded—and Wham-O Inc. was left with millions of unwanted hoops cluttering factory floors. People had decided to try something else that was cool, novel, and new. Wham-O Inc. even *lost* money in the end: $10,000. Eventually, the company went back to selling a spinning disk toy meant to cash in on the craze around flying saucers.

Maybe you've heard of it? It was called the Frisbee.

LOOK AT ME! I'M WEIRD AND DIFFERENT!

OOH LOOK AH

Here's the Story: HOBBLE SKIRTS

It's 1910 and you are excited!

Today is the high school dance and you are SO going to wear your brand-new outfit and make everyone else positively green with envy! No more cumbersome, floor-scraping skirts for you. You just spent all your money on your very own hobble skirt.

Two steps forward, one step back?

Who could blame women for wanting to try out the newest fashion fad, after years of wearing heavy, long fabrics, bustles, and petticoats? The hobble skirt was a slim, fitted skirt that probably felt fresh and modern to many wearers. Not only did it show off the shape of their legs, the skirt made women teeter around in a funny, wiggling way that some people thought looked kind of attractive.

Yet it's hard to overlook the fact that these impractical skirts made it difficult to do things as simple as running or climbing stairs. Imagine walking around with an elastic band around your calves! Why would anyone want to do that?

WHAT DOES IT ALL MEAN?

For a fad to catch on, people have to notice an item and feel drawn to it. Women began to see hobble skirts in magazine ads and catalogs, and the skirts caught their attention. Why? It turns out that nothing makes our brains happier than being presented with something weird or new. (Ugly Crocs? Check. Spinning, colorful hoops? Check.) In fact, seeking out and paying attention to new things is hardwired right into our brains.

Science experiments reveal that when people are shown pictures of oddball things they've never seen before, an area in the middle of the brain "lights up." Then a "reward chemical" called dopamine is released, which is a message from the brain telling us that the new thing could make us feel good. Suddenly, we perk up and think, "I want!" We're probably not even aware it's happening.

I want to fit in, too!

Of course, there are other, more emotional reasons people quickly jump on the bandwagon and forget common sense in order to be "fashionable." Human beings, like dogs, dolphins, and monkeys, are social mammals. **And as such, we want to…**

If you ever feel this way, you're definitely not alone. Research shows that while adults buy into trends to impress other people, kids generally follow fads because they want to fit in. That's understandable. No one wants to be left out!

But before you chase the next fashion craze, ask yourself if new clothes will actually give you the connection you crave.

CHAPTER 2

SPREAD THE WORD

Here's how fads—and the ideas and feelings that drive them—spread from person to person, city to city, and even country to country…then catch fire!

BUT FIRST...

Wild Fact! Some Fads Actually Evolve to Become Long-Term Innovations

In centuries past, most people wouldn't be caught dead wearing a clock on a bracelet. Definitely not men who preferred the traditional pocket watch.

A wristwatch—or "strap watch," as it was called then—was just a fad.

What? Wear a watch where everybody can see it? No way!

There's some excuse for a woman wearing her watch on her wrist, but a man has plenty of pockets.

Eventually, people got used to seeing wristwatches during World War I, when soldiers wore them. They were easy to check, which was more practical than rifling through pockets during battle.

Once soldiers returned home, people began to recognize the wristwatch's charms, and the fad became a trend—and eventually a useful, can't-live-without-it* innovation.

NEW! WRISTWATCHES

Sometimes fads turn into trends, which have a longer life span and can last months or years. And some of those trends will turn into what are called "classics." Wristwatches are a classic example...of a classic!

*Until the invention of the smartphone, that is.

17

SOME FADS BUILD ON WHAT CAME BEFORE

Here's the Story:
BABY NAMES

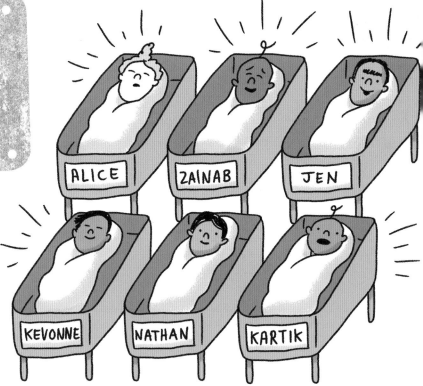

In 1936, an author named Margaret Mitchell wrote a brick of a book called *Gone with the Wind*.

It was hugely popular and won an armful of big awards. The story's main character? A young woman named Scarlett O'Hara.

You'd think parents would have been falling all over themselves to call their baby girls Scarlett. But that didn't happen. Not even when a blockbuster movie based on the book came out. The name barely cracked the "thousand most popular names" list in the United States. (Maybe because Scarlett O'Hara wasn't exactly the nicest person.)

For decades Scarlett was an uncommon name. Then suddenly, in 2016, it shot up baby name lists, making it the eighteenth most popular girl's name in the U.S.

WHAT DOES IT ALL MEAN?

Look around your classroom. How many Gertrudes, Berthas, and Ronalds can you count? Probably not many. Meanwhile, there's a good chance you've got at least one Ava, Sophia, or Ethan a few desks over. Fads and trends don't just apply to toys, hairstyles, and shoes. Names can be *hot* or *not*, too.

Experts who research fads, trends, and popularity love studying baby names because names offer insight into how popularity spreads without being influenced by outside forces like advertising, technological advances, or price differences.

In other words, all names are "worth" pretty much the same.

Even so, figuring out why some names become faddish while others remain underused is complicated. Here's what studies show…

We like to stand out (a little)

In countries that prize individualism, or standing out from the crowd, parents are more likely to choose names that are a bit different.

But here's an important key: they can't be *too* different.

That's right. According to onomastics experts (people who study names), if Emily is popular one year, new parents might give it a twist: Emma. Soon other parents are naming their girls Ella and then maybe Bella.

Which brings us back to Scarlett. Maybe its rise to sudden fame has nothing to do with the fact that new parents today have forgotten the scheming Scarlett O'Hara. Maybe they simply like it because it rhymes with another name that was trending just before it: Charlotte.

Your Little Nutella Is So Cute!

Fish and Chips. Strawberry. Talula Does the Hula From Hawaii. (Seriously.) And yep, Nutella. These are all real names parents have tried to call their kids over the years. Their attempts didn't work. When the parents tried to register their children's names, their governments said no.

MEDIA CAN TURN A FAD INTO A LASTING ICON

Here's the Story:
THE *MONA LISA* HEIST

Quick! What's the name of this painting?

Easy, right? It's the *Mona Lisa* (also known as *La Gioconda*). Believe it or not, this portrait was not always a household name. So how did its image spread to help it become the world's most famous painting?

On the morning of August 21, 1911, Vincenzo Perugia walked out of the Louvre, the famous art museum in Paris, wearing a roomy white smock—and perhaps looking a little nervous. He had every right to be. He'd just stolen the *Mona Lisa* and had it tucked inside his shirt!

It was Monday, and the museum was closed, but Perugia had been hiding in an art supply closet all night, waiting for his chance to swipe the painting. As a former gallery handyman, he knew exactly where to conceal himself.

Although art experts thought the *Mona Lisa* was a masterpiece, the painting certainly wasn't the most famous piece of art in the building at the time. However, because the portrait was small, only 30 by 21 inches (77 by 53 cm), it seemed like an easy piece to steal.

When Perugia knew the coast was clear, he unhooked the painting from the wall, removed the glass case and frame, walked out the door, and hopped on a train for home. Little did he know that by stealing the *Mona Lisa*, he would be turning it into a worldwide media sensation—and making it too well known to sell without getting caught!

WHAT DOES IT ALL MEAN?

It took twenty-six hours for anyone to even realize the painting was missing. But when word got out, the news sparked a fad—of interest, conversation, and ideas.

Not at first, though. Since most people were not familiar with the painting, police printed up thousands of flyers to show them what the *Mona Lisa* looked like. Then newspapers around the world splashed its picture across their front pages. Some even offered big rewards for the painting's return. Actors and singers dressed up as the woman in the painting, people wrote songs and sung them in cafes, and there were *Mona Lisa* jokes, riddles, and postcards, too.

Her smile sells newspapers!

Remember, this was way before twenty-four-hour news, social media, smartphones, the Internet, and even television! Yet the *Mona Lisa* went viral because newspapers and magazines turned the heist into front-page news that reached millions of people worldwide. The painting sparked the dawn of what we call the "mass-media age."

We like what we know

So why is the *Mona Lisa* still considered the best-known painting on the planet? Thank something called the **mere exposure effect**. It's a theory that suggests the more we come into contact with something, the more we like it. After the initial excitement of seeing something new, when people were repeatedly exposed to the painting's image, they started to think it was important, simply because they saw it so often.

But something else sealed the fate of the *Mona Lisa*: its disappearance, or scarcity, made the painting seem more valuable, like any other faddish collectable, such as rare stamps or, yep, a limited supply of Hula-Hoops.

Caught!!

Two years later, Perugia was finally caught trying to sell the painting in Italy and the *Mona Lisa* was returned to France. But by then, the art world had a new number-one celebrity.

Here's the Story: ANESTHESIA

100...99...98...97...zzzz...

When we go into surgery today, we expect two things:

1. We'll feel no pain.

2. We won't remember anything afterward.

It wasn't always that way. Throughout most of history, surgery was brutal. Terrified patients screamed. Others passed out from the pain. It was hard on doctors, too. Some cried or were sick because of the stress. There had to be some way to ease the misery, but no one could find anything that worked.

Step right up—this show's a gas!

That is, until an American dentist, Horace Wells, made a discovery in the weirdest place. In 1844, he shelled out twenty-five cents to watch a "laughing gas" show. Crowds actually paid to watch people inhale nitrous oxide, or laughing gas, and make fools of themselves. That day, one participant ran crazily through the theater and injured his leg. Rushing to his aid, Wells was shocked to discover the man felt no pain! Wells immediately started experimenting with the gas in his lab. Sadly, he discovered the effects didn't last long enough to be used in operations.

AAHHH!!!

No pain, all gain

Then, a breakthrough. Dr. William Morton, Wells's former student, tried another gas: ether. He designed a machine that would dole it out slowly and evenly. On October 16, 1846, he used this new invention while removing a patient's jaw tumor.

No moving. No screaming. No pain. Doctors watching the operation in the medical hall were shocked.

The idea spread like a virus! (Or at least as fast as the times allowed: it took two months by ship for the news to reach Europe.) Doctors wrote letters to other doctors. They talked about it at meetings. They published papers in medical journals, too. Despite some foot-dragging by out-of-touch surgeons who insisted pain was a necessary evil, within seven short years, anesthesia was used around the world.

WHAT DOES IT ALL MEAN?

If many fads spread through word of mouth, why do people share some ideas and not others? Why do some catch on so quickly? That's a question Jonah Berger, a marketing professor, explores. According to his research, a super "contagious" idea has to have six qualities, or **STEPPS**:

S **Social Currency: People share what makes them look good, cool, or smart.** Surgeons thought patients might see them as more intelligent and skilled if they used anesthesia.

T **Triggers: We've got to be reminded to talk about them.** Each successful (and pain-free!) surgery reminded doctors anesthesia worked.

E **Emotion: When we care, we share.** No more stress. Anesthesia made doctors happy, too!

P **Public: If we can see it, we're more likely to talk about it.** It was easy for other doctors to see ether's effects on patients when they watched surgeries, which were sometimes performed in medical halls in front of an audience of doctors.

P **Practical Value: People prefer to share helpful ideas.** This medical breakthrough was 100% useful.

S **Stories: It's got to have a great story!** Tales about happy patients were good enough to share.

Anesthesia checks every single box. Its amazing pain-squashing effects were also discovered during a time when medicine was becoming more scientific. Those medical papers raving about anesthesia certainly didn't hurt. No wonder it caught fire so quickly.

IF EVERYBODY ELSE DOES IT, IT'S OKAY, RIGHT?

BUY! BUY! BUY!! SELL!!!

Here's the Story:
STOCK MARKET CRASH

Optimistic. That's the best way to describe how a lot of people felt in the 1920s.

It was the decade known for new inventions: radios, speedy Ford automobiles, silent movies, frozen food, Band-Aids, bulldozers, and even the pop-up toaster. Talk about an era of exciting progress.

What's more? Banks made it easy to borrow money and buy all this wonderful stuff. People started investing their money in the stock market, hoping to make a fortune! They thought the good times were going to last forever…

But they didn't.

Problem was, companies had made too many products and couldn't sell them all. Eventually many people lost their jobs, making them unable to pay off their debts. Company stocks started dropping in value.

Investors—people who'd put money into those companies—started to get nervous. They sold their overpriced stocks, hoping to keep their money safe. Then other investors sold theirs, too. Hey, if so many people were selling, that must mean they knew what they were doing, right?

Then panic set in. By October 29, 1929—also known as Black Tuesday—the market went into free fall! Billions of dollars were lost.

Next stop: The Great Depression.

We call the 1929 stock market crash the collapse of a bubble. People were swept up in the craze, buying *and* selling, and then suddenly they moved on. (Sound familiar?) So why do people imitate others even when it's illogical?

WHAT DOES IT ALL MEAN?

Say you walk by two empty restaurants on the same street. You know they both serve delicious food, but you choose one over the other. No reason. Just because.

A family comes along and sees you in the restaurant. They think, "Hey, this one has people in it. It must be better than the empty one."

Then another family makes the same assumption. And another.

By the end of the night, the restaurant you chose is hopping! But the other is still empty.

What do restaurants and stock market crashes have in common?

Two words: **information cascades**. In other words, you're more likely to do something if you see other people around you doing it, too—even if there's no evidence it's a good idea. Maybe you're worried about fitting in. Or you assume that if everyone else is taking action, they know something you don't.

How Do Stocks Work?

Let's say a pencil company wants to build a new factory to make even more pencils. They sell little pieces of their company to raise money. These pieces are called stocks, and nearly anyone can buy them.

Soon the company is making more money, so its stocks are worth more. But if the pencils stop selling, the stocks lose their value.

We buy and sell stocks (or shares) on the stock market.

Psst! Pass it on

We're constantly picking up information and ideas from the people around us and using it to help us decide how to act. In fact, this pattern is a driving force in our lives and it's the reason why the Swiss act Swiss, the Japanese act Japanese, the Americans act American, and the Kenyans act Kenyan. Information cascades also partly explain why people jump on bandwagons and follow silly fads.

MADE, NOT BORN

Some flash-in-the-pan fads are not so out-of-the-blue after all. They're carefully and painstakingly crafted to make us want to jump on board, change our behavior—and even convince others to join in, too.

BUT FIRST...

Yes, You Can Start a Fad
(With Sneaky Help You're Probably Unaware Of)

Say hi to Hannah. She's like a lot of kids in her town.

Next week is her eighth grade graduation, and it's almost like someone out there knows what's going on in her life. Creepy...

The truth: Every computer click and keystroke Hannah makes is collected and stored by BIG DATA companies. Sometimes they sell that info to other companies to create super-targeted online advertisements just for her.

It's called predictive marketing—ad companies try to predict what you'll want to buy before you even know yourself!

But those billions of tiny pieces of online information from millions of people are used to create more than just ads. They can be analyzed to generate something even more far-reaching: fads.

Let's say Hannah and another million kids start searching for the word "pineapple." Companies track these searches. And—ka-ching!

Now pineapples are everywhere! By tracking what Hannah and billions of other people do online today, companies can use what they know about us to manufacture the fads of tomorrow. Eek!

I LIKE IT BECAUSE IT'S (ALREADY) POPULAR!

Here's the Story:
THE PAYOLA SCANDAL

Twenty-two thousand dollars. That's how much money a radio deejay, Phil Lind, said he'd taken as a bribe to play a record on the radio.

It was 1959, and rock 'n' roll was in its heyday. Kids and teens were snatching up record singles like "Turn Me Loose" and "Personality." Top 40 music ruled the airwaves.

But record companies had a serious dilemma. At a time when they produced literally hundreds of singles a week, how could they ensure their songs would be played on the radio? And even if they did get airtime, how could they help turn one of their songs into a hit—a fad in the music world?

Easy. They'd buy their way in.

This form of bribery—paying a radio station money to play your song—is called payola. The "Payola Scandal" of the 1950s ended with companies being fined and radio deejays getting fired. One legendary deejay, Alan Freed, who coined the term "rock 'n' roll," never worked in radio again. When he died a few years later, he was broke and angry.

WHAT DOES IT ALL MEAN?

There was a good reason record companies were so tempted to flash some cash in order to get their songs on the radio. They knew something weird about how songs actually become popular hits: the more we hear a song, the more we think we like it.

Even today, with so many online options for finding new music—Spotify, Apple Music, YouTube, and musicians' own websites—the best way to create a hit is to get it played, played, and played again on the radio. At least until there's a tipping point and the song becomes *too* familiar. Then it's no longer special, exclusive, and cool.

There's a name for our preference for things we recognize: the mere exposure effect. (Remember the *Mona Lisa* back on page 20? The effect works with music, too.)

Um, didn't I just see that?

Back in the 1960s, a psychologist named Robert Zajonc conducted a series of experiments. He showed people a stack of silly nonsense words and weird shapes and letters. Sometimes they saw an image only once or twice. Other images showed up again and again. Then Zajonc asked them which ones they liked best. Almost without fail, people chose the characters and shapes they'd seen most often. They preferred them, not because triangles are necessarily better than squares, but because they knew the triangles better.

Whether you're trying to craft a music hit, food fad, or toy craze, you've got to give it one thing: exposure.

29

WITH THE RIGHT AD, THEY'LL EAT IT UP

Here's the Story: FONDUE

Ooey, gooey, squishy, and warm. It's hard not to love cheese fondue.

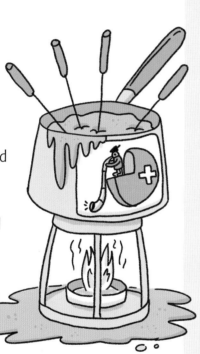

No wonder everyone seemed to have a fondue pot tucked away in their kitchen in the 1960s and 1970s. Yet if you'd asked them why, most people probably had no idea. A likely explanation? Their friends had one.

Whatever the reason, there was no denying fondue came at the perfect time. Fancy and formal dinner parties of the 1950s? No thanks. The '60s and '70s were all about being casual and relaxed. And nothing reflected that social trend more than digging in and eating from the same communal dish.

WHAT DOES IT ALL MEAN?

Here's a secret: The fondue fad didn't just happen by accident. It was actually carefully planned and manufactured by a powerful group in Switzerland, the Swiss Cheese Union.

No. Not the dreaded Swiss Cheese Union!

It's true. This group of cheese makers—some call it a cartel—had total control over the country's large cheese industry for eighty-five years. It told cheese makers what kinds of cheese they could make and sell, and how much they could export to other countries.

Eventually, the Union declared that fondue, a little-known regional recipe from the mountainous Alps area, would be the country's national dish. It was a smart, if devilish, move. Fondue is literally a big, mouthwatering bowl of melted cheese made from Emmental and Gruyère cheeses—the two main types the Union wanted more people to buy!

To get the word out, the Union created slogans for advertising posters ("Fondue creates a good mood!") and even sent fondue sets to the military.

Then the Union started to look for new customers across the ocean.

Wanted: More cheese slurpers!

The United States was one of the biggest cheese markets in the world, and the Swiss Cheese Union wanted in. But how to get Americans to slurp cheese by the bowlfuls? Since advertising and marketing worked on the Swiss, the Union used the same tactics to create demand for its cheese.

The first ads were a bit scary, though.

These stern advertisements didn't work well on the Americans, who were much more accustomed to upbeat ads that made them feel good about themselves and life in general. A different culture required a different approach.

It's all about how you spin it

But then came a stroke of advertising genius years later: The Union started running ads that seemed downright fun. These new advertisements showed crowds of healthy, hearty Swiss skiers in the Alps laughing together over a bubbling pot of cheese. These new ads placed the focus on the people rather than the food. They were selling a fun, exciting lifestyle—that anyone could have if they just ate fondue!

There's no denying that the Swiss Cheese Union's ads worked a miracle and created a fad from scratch. By using effective advertising and marketing tactics, it was able to plant a powerful idea in people's minds: melted cheese isn't just delicious—it will make you happier, healthier, and even more popular!

Who would say no to *that*?

That is, until another trend surfaced: low fat. And faster than you can say "great globs of grease," the fondue fad was over.

MANUFACTURED FADS NEED WORD-OF-MOUTH BUZZ

Here's the Story:
UNICORN FOOD

Question: What looks like a unicorn, smells like a unicorn, and tastes like a unicorn?

Answer: Back in 2017, Starbucks, the popular coffee chain, unleashed a new drink fad almost as awe-inspiring as any magical creature—a fairy-hued concoction sprinkled with "pixie powder dust." It was called the Unicorn Frappuccino and touted as being "fleeting as a rainbow." (In other words, it would only be available from April 19 to 23.)

Days before the official launch, Starbucks not-so-secretly leaked photos of the drink on social media, and soon coffee fans were raving.

Then came the launch. The Unicorn "Frap" was blue and pink all right. It was also lip-puckeringly sweet —with a whopping 14.5 teaspoons of sugar in a 16-ounce drink! But buyers didn't care. Many stores ran out of ingredients within a day. Lucky sippers snapped pictures and posted them online.

Not everyone thought the drink was worth the attention, though.

"To be clear, this is the worst drink I have ever purchased in my life," wrote one reporter in the U.S.

"It tastes like orange Trident gum and hot dog water. Don't waste your money on it!" implored a Twitter user.

But as far as Starbucks was concerned, their manufactured food fad was a success. Love it or hate it, the Unicorn Frap got the world talking about its coffee shop brand.

WHAT DOES IT ALL MEAN?

Here's the thing. Word-of-mouth is ten times more successful than advertising when it comes to creating hoopla. Research shows people trust other people, not companies. The Starbucks marketing people probably knew this fact, so they set out to generate word-of-mouth buzz between friends and social media followers online. Here's how:

1. They piggybacked on existing trends.

People were already posting food pictures from their phones and computers, the more colorful and outrageous the better. Starbucks also knew that magical animals were trending on social media. They even admit that's where they got their idea.

2. They made it Instagrammable.

A picture is worth a thousand words, right? The colorful Unicorn Frap wasn't really meant to be enjoyed—but to be shared online.

3. They made it scarce.

People want what they can't have. Not only does scarcity make something seem more valuable, but it sets off a competitive streak in us. (You got your hands on the drink? You didn't just buy it, you *won* it!) Scarcity also drives us to fear we're missing out.

4. They made it for you.

Yep, you. There wasn't any coffee in the kid-appealing drink. That way Starbucks could market it to kids and teens, too. They were probably hoping if new, young customers came to Starbucks, they would turn into fans for life.

Just so you know.

WE DON'T FOLLOW TRENDS, WE FOLLOW THE COOL PEOPLE WHO START THEM

Here's the Story: SLIME!

In a nutshell, here's what you need to make your own slime:

1. White glue
2. Baking soda
3. Contact lens solution

Simple. Except the slime fad a few years ago proved to be a very big deal—to the tune of $200,000!

Rolling in dough

That's how much money American YouTube and Instagram queen Karina Garcia said she was making "in a really good month" by posting online videos of herself whipping up gobs of fluffy, glittery, or stretchy goo. She didn't have to sell it, either. According to news reports at the time, Garcia was receiving sponsorship cash from big companies like Coca-Cola and Disney.

No wonder they wanted to advertise with her. Garcia's videos and photos attracted millions of views. Her most popular, called "100 Lbs of Slime!," got over twenty-one million hits! At the fad's height, she was able to buy a house with a pool for her family.

Goo isn't new

Slime has been popular before, probably because a lot of kids make it for the first time at school in science class. But social media quickly helped turn slime into a "thing."

For months, kids were making videos of themselves poking, squishing, and stretching colorful, glittery slime. Others were selling it online for five, ten, or twenty-five dollars per tub. The Instagram hashtag #slime appeared nearly seven million times that year. Stores even ran out of Elmer's Glue, a slime ingredient, and the company had to ramp up production.

But by the end of 2017, slime slumped, and kids went online looking for new crafts to try.

WHAT DOES IT ALL MEAN?

Unlike the Frappuccino fad on the previous page, the slime fad rose up because kids just like you decided that something—and someone—was cool and then, thanks to technology, spread the word!

What makes someone follow-worthy and cool?

It's a great question. It's also one advertising people would kill for the answer to, because fads and trends often start with just one or two influential kids or adults. These people are key to making word-of-mouth catch fire! (Hey, we don't always know what's cool, but we know *who's* cool, right? It's easier to just follow their lead.)

It turns out there are **two types** of cool people, at least according to Australian researchers:

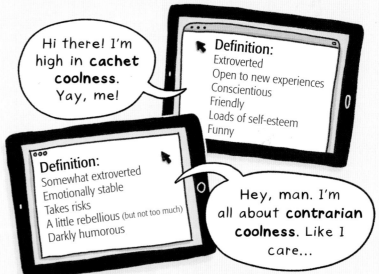

Hi there! I'm high in **cachet coolness**. Yay, me!

Definition:
Extroverted
Open to new experiences
Conscientious
Friendly
Loads of self-esteem
Funny

Definition:
Somewhat extroverted
Emotionally stable
Takes risks
A little rebellious (but not too much)
Darkly humorous

Hey, man. I'm all about **contrarian coolness**. Like I care...

Even though social media sites make it easy for companies to craft fads, these sites also give kids a way to find cachet and contrarian trendsetters all around the world. Now fads can pop up practically anywhere on earth—at the same time!

BAD FADS

Some fads and trends are no laughing matter. In fact, they can have serious, long-lasting, and even dangerous effects on the people drawn into a mania—not to mention those who get caught in the aftermath.

Fads Gone Wrong

Who doesn't love to dance? In the 1920s, young people joined popular **dance marathons** hoping to win much-needed cash rewards. Some shuffled for weeks. Exhausted dancers collapsed, and a few even died.

Would you gulp down a live goldfish? How about fifteen? **Goldfish-swallowing** fad = gross. One politician in 1939 called it "cruel and wanton" consumption. Gulp.

Blech. Cabbage soup. Day in and day out. At the height of the silly **Cabbage Soup Diet** craze in the 1950s, some half-starved people felt really sick!

Speaking of cabbage...**Cabbage Patch dolls** were funny looking, smelled like baby powder, and were so popular in 1983, parents started fistfighting over them in stores.

Warning! **Laundry detergent pods** are for laundry, *not* eating. Sheesh. In 2018, so many kids were licking and chewing these poisonous packets as a dumb and dangerous Internet fad, stores locked them up.

Maybe not dangerous but definitely disturbing: In the 1970s, people starting running through crowds naked—to protest something, to get publicity, or just as a silly prank. It was called the **streaking epidemic**.
And thankfully it's (mostly) over.

SOME FADS TURN INTO DANGEROUS, COSTLY OBSESSIONS

Here's the Story: BEANIE BABIES

Back in 1998, a masked man walked into a gift shop in California and told the employees to get down. He had a gun!

The thief wasn't there for the money—he actually strode right past the cash register, ignoring the bills inside. Instead, he'd come for something far more valuable: Beanie Babies.

It's a Beaniemania bubble!

This robbery happened at the height of the Beanie Baby craze of the late 1990s. Within a few short years, what started out as a collectible stuffed-animal pastime somehow took a very dark turn.

At first the beanbag toys appealed to kids. Beanies were small, only five dollars apiece, with names like "Blackie the Bear" and "Halo." Then their popularity exploded. Not just with children but with adults, too.

Newspapers ran unbelievable stories about thirteen-year-olds making over a million dollars by selling their collections. Moms bought them by the carload. A super-rare Beanie Baby sold for $10,000 on eBay. One family even sank $100,000 into the stuffed animals—and spent all the money they'd saved for their kids' college education. Meanwhile, a man in West Virginia *murdered* his coworker over a Beanie Baby deal gone wrong.

The fad eventually tanked—and today millions of worthless Beanie Babies have been abandoned to basements and trash cans.

WHAT DOES IT ALL MEAN?

Ty Warner, the mastermind behind Beanie Babies, knew how to create a toy fad frenzy by manipulating supply and demand. He created novelty by introducing new toys—and he created scarcity by "retiring" others.

The scheme worked too well, though.

One former salesperson later described Beanie Babies to a reporter as *"something really cute that just brought out the worst in people."*

The worst…as in grown-ups ruining things for kids?

Yep. Beanie Babies probably would have gone the way of most other kids' fads: boom, bust, and on to the next silly (and usually inexpensive) thing. But that's not what happened. Instead, the fad went dangerously haywire because greedy adults turned cute stuffed animals for kids into a way to make money for themselves. Beanie Babies were treated like currency and the fad went from a fun pastime to a hazardous obsession for those who got caught up in the bubble. In fact, some people would call this extreme fad a "craze" or even a "mania."

ma·ni·a (noun): periods of great excitement, extreme enthusiasm, euphoria, delusions, and overactivity.

Gambling rarely pays off

Get-rich-quick schemes are about taking risks and hoping they'll pay off. And for a few people, they do. Yet for the majority, gambling just leads to an empty wallet. What's more, about 2% of those who gamble become addicted—always looking for the next "win" (or in this case, rare Beanie Baby)—and can't stop until they've lost everything. Not exactly child's play.

FOOD FADS LEAVE FARMERS IN THE LURCH

Here's the Story: QUINOA

Mom! Can you buy me some Ancient Grains Super-Mega Blast™? Pleeeeze?

Okay, maybe you would never really beg for a breakfast cereal made of spelt, amaranth, millet, and brown rice. Yet back in 2015, if you'd wandered the grocery aisles, you likely would have noticed so-called "ancient grains" sprouting up in everything from waffles to chocolate chip cookies.

It's a bird, it's a grain…it's superfood!

The ancient grain fad blended perfectly with an even bigger food trend: healthy eating. Grains like kamut or brown rice were thought to be better than plain old white rice. Some even called the most popular grain, quinoa (pronounced KEEN-wa), a "superfood" due to its small, nutritious seeds.

Even though farmers have grown quinoa for thousands of years in the Andes Mountains of South America, when a few high-end restaurants in North America started using it in recipes, word got out. Food bloggers started writing about it. TV shows spread the word further. Eventually, quinoa popped up on casual restaurant menus and grocery store shelves.

Production quadrupled between 2008 and 2014. By then it was a full-fledged fad.

WHAT DOES IT ALL MEAN?

"Fad." If you're a farmer, it's a bad word. That's because farmers must plan ahead and make plenty of educated guesses. Plant soybeans or corn? Two fields or three? What crop will be most in demand next year? The fickleness of fads—particularly those that last only a few months—can lead to financial disaster...

Back in the 1980s, a hundred pounds of quinoa, a staple of the local diet in South America, wouldn't have earned enough money to buy a pair of jeans.

But then fancy-pants restaurants in the U.S. start serving the ancient grain. **It's a revelation!** Interest starts to grow...and grow.

Hello, quinoa fad. Prices soar and farmers in the Andes Mountains make serious dough. They update their houses. Buy tractors.

Farmers in other countries look at quinoa profits and say, "Hmm. Maybe I should grow that, too."

Now Andes farm fields are no longer as rich and fertile as before. There's so much demand, farmers aren't letting field soil go fallow (or rest).

With so much quinoa grown globally, there's a glut. Prices drop. Andes farmers struggle. Some are ruined because they've devoted their farms to quinoa. They have no Plan B.

Now there's buzz about the next big North American food fad—bug protein!

41

Here's the Story:
THE VACCINE SCANDAL

You can get a lot of things at theme parks. Funnel cakes. Goofy-looking hats. A tummy ache from spinning rides.

But in early 2015, 147 visitors to Disneyland in California reportedly ended up with something else entirely: measles.

The outbreak was a big deal because measles was supposed to be eliminated in the United States—mostly due to a vaccine introduced in 1963.

Ouch!

Of course no one *likes* getting shots at the doctor's office, but shots are lifesavers. Literally. Before the measles vaccine (called MMR), three to four million people in the U.S. were infected each year. Measles sent forty-eight thousand people to the hospital and even caused between four hundred and five hundred deaths! The vaccine made those numbers nearly disappear.

Vaccinated people = no way for the virus to spread.

Bad science

So how did measles spread at Disneyland years later? Back up to 1998. That's when a doctor named Andrew Wakefield made a scary announcement: Vaccines weren't safe after all. They were linked to autism, he said.

The news media went nuts, and some celebrities jumped on the bandwagon, helping spread the idea that vaccines were poisoning kids! Many parents worried and stopped vaccinating their babies or put shots off a little longer.

Here's the kicker

Wakefield's research was bogus. More than a dozen studies around the world have since roundly debunked his claims, and now Wakefield isn't even allowed to be a doctor anymore.

His research paper has been described as "perhaps the most damaging medical hoax of the last 100 years."

WHAT DOES IT ALL MEAN?

The anti-vaccination movement followed the trajectory of a fad. It quickly took off with some help from trendsetters—celebrities—and then faded. Except it didn't. Not entirely anyway. Some people still think vaccines cause autism despite evidence that this was never true at all.

Weird? Sure is. But people's decisions are often tainted by what we call **behavioral biases**. We simply have a hard time making rational decisions because all kinds of emotions get in the way. This illogical thinking is part of being human and why, when people argue, they usually don't change their minds, even if the other person makes persuasive points. Hey, who wants to admit to being wrong?

Take the **backfire effect**. It describes instances when our deepest beliefs are questioned and we stick to our guns even more!

> It's supposed to look like this!

Or there's the **sunk cost fallacy**. That's when people have invested a lot of time, money, or effort into something and feel they have to continue what they're doing—even if it no longer makes sense. Dignity (not to mention time and effort) is on the line here!

The problem with keeping the anti-vaccination trend alive is that it can continue to hurt those we love.

(Not So) Expert Advice

? If most actors, singers, and YouTubers don't have a medical background, why do so many people take their nonsense health advice?

1. Their ideas stand out, even if they're false. We simply notice them more.

2. They have "cool" traits, so we want to be like them. ("That hair, those teeth, that cockamamie idea…")

3. We're more likely to trust people we think we "know," even if we've never actually met them in person.

DANGEROUS IDEAS CAN ALSO BE MARKETED

Here's the Story:

MALICIOUS PROPAGANDA

If you had been a kid in Germany in the 1930s, there's a chance you would have come across a book called *The Poisonous Mushroom*. Or maybe another one, *Trust No Fox*.

The titles were grim—but the books were also dangerous. They were Nazi propaganda meant to quickly turn white Christian kids against their Jewish neighbors, shop owners, piano teachers, and even friends.

What Is Propaganda?

It's a message with one very specific goal: to spread misinformation, half-truths, and lies so its audience will adopt new—and sometimes dangerous—beliefs.

Fast and furious

Nazis wrongly believed Jews wanted to take over the country. And publishing mean-spirited books wasn't the only way the Nazis tried to change opinion and spark a flurry of anti-Semitic (anti-Jewish) feelings in the years leading up to World War II.

They published newspapers, produced films, and sold extremely cheap radios so everyone could listen to propaganda newscasts. They plastered posters in shops, squares, and churches that showed strong men holding flags, happy families hugging, and even Hitler picking up and cuddling little kids. "Children, What Do You Know about Your Leader?" read one poster.

The posters were simple, bold, and sadly—like the rest of the malicious propaganda—they worked.

44

No escape

Millions of German children and youth actually discovered Nazi ideas in their classrooms. New textbooks taught racism, anti-Semitism, and absolute obedience. There were also school political "clubs." In January 1933, the Hitler Youth group had fifty thousand members. Three years later, there were 5.4 million kids and teens taking part in after-school meetings, sports teams, rallies, and even weekend camping trips.

The Nazis used these clubs to spread their hateful ideas and encourage members to pull in their friends.

At the end of the war, young Germans were required to undergo a "de-Nazification" process to help them recover from the effects of twelve years of Nazi propaganda.

WHAT DOES IT ALL MEAN?

Propaganda can have disastrous results. Six million Jews were murdered by the Nazis. Other vulnerable people were killed, too.

And although it's easy to assume that typical Germans were simply brainwashed into going along with the insanity, the reasons few people resisted are complicated. Ultimately, the Nazi propaganda machine delivered a message that many—especially millions of unemployed, poor, or powerless people—wanted to hear:

"You deserve better. You matter. Other people are to blame for your misfortune."

How Can You Tell It's Propaganda?

It uses name-calling. "He's stingy, a traitor, crooked, and dangerous!"

It encourages the bandwagon effect. "Hey, side with us. Everybody else has!"

It uses vague but promising "glitter" words. "Freedom! Dreams! Family!"

CONCLUSION

Do Some Good

By now you know that not all fads are harmless. In fact, between manufactured advertising buzz, idea pushing, and trendspotting, you might worry you're being manipulated without even realizing it. But here's the thing. You can actually use your insider knowledge about fads to make the world a better, kinder, and happier place!

Spread useful and uplifting advice

Jamie Oliver, a famous chef in the U.K. who is known all around the world, has dedicated a lot of his time, passion, and money to spreading the word about homemade, healthy, tasty food. He gets kids involved, too. As a well-known celebrity, he's using his own mere exposure effect to do good.

Use social media to help people change their ways for the better

Back in 2010, researchers in the U.S. created a study that targeted sixty-one million Facebook users. On the same day as a congressional election, some people saw an "I Voted" button pop up on their feed. They were supposed to click it to tell their friends they'd gone to the polls. Some also saw photos of friends who'd clicked the button. The result? They were more likely to vote compared to people who didn't get the message. As long as personal information is used properly by social media companies, the bandwagon effect can do a lot of good!

Turn charitable giving into the next trending sensation and save lives

That's exactly what happened with the "Ice Bucket Challenge" back in the summer of 2014. People dumped freezing cold ice water over their heads for charity, shared videos of their stunt online—and invited other friends to do the same. The fad raised over $115 million for the ALS Association, which funds research and aid for people with Lou Gehrig's disease. Two years later, scientists discovered a new gene tied to the condition.

Give old fads new life

Some former Beanie Baby collectors have started donating thousands of perfectly preserved critters to children's hospitals, police departments, and even the military. Nurses, police officers, and soldiers give them to scared little kids at home and in war-torn countries. Even if the toys are no longer worth millions, they're still really cute!

See? Fads and trends—and how they spread lightning fast—are anything but silly, frivolous, or flip. For better or for worse, they have the power to change lives.

INDEX

SELECTED SOURCES

Bartholomew, Robert E., and Peter Hassall. *A Colorful History of Popular Delusions*. Amherst, NY: Prometheus Books, 2015.

Berger, Jonah. *Contagious: Why Things Catch On*. New York, NY: Simon & Schuster, 2013.

Berger, Jonah. *Invisible Influence: The Hidden Forces That Shape Behavior*. New York, NY: Simon & Schuster, 2017.

Best, Joel. *Flavor of the Month: Why Smart People Fall for Fads*. Oakland, CA: University of California Press, 2006.

Bissonnette, Zac. *The Great Beanie Baby Bubble: Mass Delusion and the Dark Side of Cute*. New York, NY: Penguin Publishing Group, 2015.

Duhigg, Charles. "The Rise of the Fidget Spinner and the Fall of the Well-Managed Fad." *The New York Times Magazine*, 20 Aug. 2017, p. 12.

Gladwell, Malcolm. *The Tipping Point: How Little Things Can Make a Big Difference*. New York, NY: Little, Brown and Company, 2006.

Hevesi, Dennis. "The Inspired, the Silly and the Useless." *The New York Times*, 13 Nov., 1987, National Edition, Section B.

Laermer, Richard. *Trendspotting: Think Forward, Get Ahead, and Cash in on the Future*. New York, NY: Perigee Trade, 2002.

Laldee, Tamika S. "Fads and Children: The Early Culture of Consumption." *Syracuse University Honors Program Capstone Projects*, 632, 2006. Online.

Letscher, Martin G. "How to Tell Fads from Trends." *American Demographics*, vol. 16, no. 12, 1994, pp. 38-45.

Nguyen, Dao. "What Makes Something Go Viral?" Lecture presented as part of TED Salon event, in partnership with Brightline Initiative, New York City, NY: October 2017. Online.

Sohn, Emily. "Why Do Children Love Those Fad Toys So?" *Shots: Health News from NPR*. 10 May 2017. Online.

"Antisemitism: The Longest Hatred." *Confront Hatred and Antisemitism*, United States Holocaust Memorial Museum. Online.